THE STRENGTH
OF THESE ARMS

LIFE IN THE SLAVE QUARTERS

RAYMOND BIAL

Houghton Mifflin Company
Boston

Acknowledgments

This book would not have been possible without the hard work of a number of individuals and institutions dedicated to preserving and restoring many African-American historical sites. I would particularly like to thank the staff at Carter Grove Plantation, Monticello, Boone Hall Plantation, the Old Slave House, the Hermitage, Stone Mountain, and Magnolia Plantation for permission to photograph at their historical sites. My appreciation also goes to the J. Paul Getty Museum, Penn School, the Southern Historical Collection at the University of North Carolina, Historic Stagville, and the Illinois State Historical Society for making available a number of photographs and illustrations for this book.

I would like to extend warmest thanks to my editor, Audrey Bryant, for ably guiding this project from concept to finished book. As always, I would like to thank my wife, Linda, and my children, Anna, Sarah, and Luke, for their inspiration and support.

Copyright © 1997 by Raymond Bial

The text of this book is set in 14 point Goudy.
Book design by S. M. Sherman, Ars Agassiz, Cambridge, Massachusetts.

Library of Congress Cataloging-in-Publication Data

    Bial, Raymond.
    The strength of these arms : life in the slave quarters / by Raymond Bial.
    p. cm.
    Summary: Describes how slaves were able to preserve some elements of their African heritage despite the often brutal treatment they experienced on Southern plantations.
    ISBN 0-395-77394-6
    1. Slavery — Southern States — History — Juvenile literature. 2. Slaves — Southern States — Social conditions — Juvenile literature. 3. Afro-Americans — Southern States — Social conditions — Juvenile literature. 4. Afro-Americans — Southern States — Social life and customs — Juvenile literature. 5. Plantation life — Southern States — History — Juvenile literature. 6. Southern States — Social conditions — Juvenile literature. [1. Slavery — Southern States — History. 2. Slaves — Social life and customs. 3. Plantation life. 4. Southern States — History.] I. Title.
    E443.B46 1997
    975'.00496073 — dc21   96-39860
                                                                  CIP AC

Printed in Singapore
TWP 10 9 8 7 6 5 4

This book is respectfully dedicated to the millions of people—men, women, and children—who struggled with strength and dignity against the outrageous institution of slavery.

Over the years, descriptions of plantation life have usually focused on the privileged lives of the owners who lived in the "big house," as the mansion was called. Books and movies such as *Gone with the Wind* have offered a romantic view of the Old South but a false one, with regard to both slaves and owners. Few masters were high-minded, and no slaves were happy with their fate. As Delia Garlic, a former slave, said, "It's bad to belong to folks that own you soul and body; that can tie you up to a tree, with your face to the tree and your arms fastened tight around it; who take a long, curling whip and cut the blood every lick." What has too often been overlooked in accounts of plantation life is the strength and dignity with which those in bondage struggled against the institution of slavery for more than 250 years. As the author Ralph Ellison pointed out, African Americans didn't simply react against slavery but

Born into slavery, children grew up poor and hungry. Dressed in rags, these two boys could hope for little more than a life of hard labor and few rewards.
Courtesy, Southern Historical Collection at the University of North Carolina and Penn School

Although slaves were allowed few possessions, they often tried to make their cabins into homes. Sometimes photographs of family members and other loved ones lined log walls.

made lives for themselves despite oppressive, often brutal conditions. As a people, they "helped create themselves out of what they found around themselves."

It is now being recognized that even under intolerable conditions, slaves were able to preserve some elements of their African heritage, having brought with them many skills, traditions of dance and music, and a rich history of storytelling. Many kidnapped Africans refused to learn English and stead-

fastly followed their religious beliefs, especially Muslims. Recent excavations of slave quarters at sites throughout the South have uncovered artifacts such as cowrie shells, which were used as money in Africa, pottery in African styles, and forked sticks hidden in walls, which was an African practice to ward off witches. These finds provide growing evidence that slaves not only resisted European

In digs like this one, of a slave cabin at the Hermitage, Andrew Jackson's home in Nashville, Tennessee, archaeologists have learned a great deal about how slaves made lives for themselves.
Courtesy, The Hermitage, Nashville, Tennessee

The stairs of the Old Slave House in Illinois were climbed by untold numbers of recaptured slaves. Runaways were imprisoned in small, barred cells in the attic before they were sent south.

influence but persisted in keeping alive many links with their African past. Combining native culture with that of their captors, generations of slaves made lives for themselves in this country despite conditions intended to destroy their very identity. Even though held in bondage, they also influenced American life as a whole, especially in the South. African-American women raised the plantation owners' children, often nursing them as babies and forming bonds that could last a lifetime. And many African words, such as *banjo, cola, tote, okay, gumbo, mumbo-jumbo, yam, okra, juke, chigger,* and *goober,* have become part of the English language.

When the first Africans arrived at the colony of Jamestown, Virginia, in 1619, they were bewildered and terrified, having been snatched from their homes, jammed into cargo holds, and carried across the vast seas to a strange land. Bound in chains and beaten by men speaking an unfamiliar language, many Africans died on the Middle Passage, as the journey across the Atlantic Ocean came to be called. "I used to sit on Grandma's lap and she told me about how they used to catch people in Africa," Luke D. Dixon remembered. "They herded them like cattle and put them in stalls and brought them on ships and sold them." The survivors were sold as slaves at auctions in seaport cities such as Newport News, Virginia, where Dixon's grandmother was bought: "It was hard on the Africans to be treated like animals. They sold Grandma's daughter to somebody in Texas. She cried and begged to let them be together. They didn't pay no attention to her."

Many kidnapped Africans fought back, but revolts were severely punished with whipping, branding, or mutilation. Alone, in couples, or in small groups, slaves sometimes escaped and hid in remote places such as the Florida Everglades and the Dismal Swamp of North Carolina and Virginia. Called maroons, these African Americans made their

Fleeing slaves were usually hunted down and recaptured, even when they hid in cypress swamps like this one in South Carolina.

homes in the woods and swamps of the South. Later, slaves fled to Canada via what became known as the Underground Railroad. Though resistance to slavery began as soon as the first captive Africans set foot on American soil and continued until the end of the Civil War, runaways were ruthlessly hunted down. Most were recaptured and forced to return to labor against their will.

Slaves were mainly used on the large farms called plantations, which gradually spread across the South from the Atlantic Ocean to the land that is now Texas. Over time several kinds of plantations evolved, each growing a different crop. The coastal plantations stretching from the Chesapeake Bay in Maryland south to Florida grew rice in carefully flooded fields. Cotton was raised in sprawling fields along a fifty-mile-wide belt that curved from the middle of South Carolina down through Georgia and Alabama to eastern Mississippi. The third plantation region, where sugar was grown, extended along the Mississippi River from just above Memphis to below New Orleans. Tobacco was also widely grown on farms in Virginia, Maryland, and Kentucky.

In 1808, Congress passed a law prohibiting the import of any more kidnapped Africans, and plantation owners began to raise another crop—

Slaves were routinely auctioned off like animals at this slave market, now preserved as a museum, in the heart of Charleston, South Carolina.

the slaves themselves. This law, intended as a step toward the gradual elimination of slavery, only served to cut off one supply of slaves and pave the way for the production of children for the auction block. Slaves on farms where slaves were bred might have received better care than those who merely worked, but only because of their value as a product. As the Virginia slave Joseph Holmes recalled, "Old Miss never allowed no mistreating the slaves. They was raising slaves for the market, and it wouldn't be good business to mistreat them." Delia Garlic remembered bitterly, "Babies was snatched from their mother's breast and sold to speculators. Chilluns was separated from sisters and brothers and never saw each other again. Course they cry! You

Slave children belonged to the master, not their mother and father. Young ones could be sold away at any time, and the parents were unable to do anything to save their children from the auction block.

On this plantation near Nashville, Tennessee, the residents enjoyed all the comforts of their wealth, including a spacious mansion surrounded by live oak trees. All the labor was provided by slaves.

think they not cry when they was sold like cattle? I could tell you about it all day, but even then you couldn't guess the awfulness of it." And sales didn't happen only on breeding farms. Masters throughout the South sold slaves, breaking up families without a second thought. They also controlled slaves with the threat of sale, especially the threat that the slaves would be "sold South," where the work in cotton fields was brutal and there was little chance of escape. Some slaves were auctioned off to settle an estate or a debt—and this happened often. The auction block was so much a part of slave life that Henry Johnson described himself as born in Virginia, raised all over the state, and "sold only twice."

What was the daily life of the slaves who actually built the big house and everything else on the plantation? On the most basic level, they were held against their will and mistreated by people who had absolute control over them—and such power often brought out the worst in a master or mistress. Masters regularly inflicted severe punishment, either directly or through an overseer or "whipping man" described by slaves as "mean as the devil." A former slave named Sara Colquitt recalled, "Our overseer was Mr. Green Ross, and he was a bad one, too.

Slaves slept either on the dirt floors of their cabins or in rough beds covered with patchwork quilts. Often, both the beds and the quilts were made by their own hands.

Slaves worked hard to keep their cabins clean and tidy, adding curtains and other improvements when they could.

Mean, my goodness! He'd whip you in a minute." Yet many slaves withstood this abuse with a burning sense of indignation or defiantly fought back. One, William H. Heard, explained that despite the worst beatings, "many of them refused to be conquered." William Wells Brown, a runaway slave, told of one powerful man who declared that "no white man should ever whip him—that he would die first."

Slaves also saw a world of difference between the wealth and luxury of the big house—which they made possible—and the stark poverty of the quarters where they lived. They were outraged that they did all the work, mostly as field hands, and the masters enjoyed all the comforts. They were denied material goods, and little money or effort was spent on them. Young boys and girls wore only long cotton shirts that hung down to their knees, while older boys and men had coarse shirts and breeches made by slave women. Women's dresses were colored with dyes from berries and nuts but otherwise plain. Once a year slaves might be allowed one or two new sets of clothes, and perhaps a new blanket. They sometimes wore crude shoes made from leather tanned on the plantation, but often went barefoot, even in winter. Yet wherever they could, slaves expressed their independence by keeping elements of African dress. Many young women wore

Plantation bedrooms were often sumptuous, especially when contrasted with the stark living conditions of the quarters

Slaves shivered in the winds that whistled through their rough cabin walls while the owners enjoyed comfortable evenings by a warm fire in their plantation homes.

beaded necklaces called charm strings to bring good luck. Occasionally men braided their hair in plaits similar to African cornrows and women tied their hair with string and bits of cloth in African styles. Most of the women and some of the men wore head kerchiefs similar to those worn in Africa. Along the

Mississippi River, head cloths like the turbans of West Africa were popular.

Slaves lived in rough one-room cabins or shacks, sometimes with as many as ten or twelve people sharing each small cabin. As Sara Colquitt said, "Us lived in log cabins with dirt floors, and they was built in two long rows. Us beds was nailed to the wall at one end, and us used corn shucks and pine straw for mattresses." Many of the cabins had no chinking between the logs, and the winter winds whistled through the cracks. They typically had few or no furnishings, yet women cleaned, cooked, and

The masters enjoyed every luxury in their homes, while those who made it possible lived in miserable conditions.

generally tried to make a home for their children. Men made tables, chairs, beds, and other furniture as well as cooking utensils. By making their cabins more livable, slaves showed that they were neither property nor work animals but human beings entitled to homes of their own. As in Africa, those who worked hard to provide for their families were highly regarded within the slave community.

Though slaves seldom ate well, they were given enough cornbread, fat pork, molasses, and sometimes coffee to work in the fields. On some plantations they sat down to meals in a dining hall, but on others they scooped food out of troughs with wooden spoons. Children were often fed only a mixture of cornbread and milk. Field hands typically received three pounds of pork a week, and the smokehouse larder was often used to control the slaves, since good workers were given more food. Yet slaves provided for themselves too, sometimes raising their own cabbage, collards, turnips, peanuts, and corn in garden plots by their cabins. They also hunted in the woods and fished in the creek, or kept a few chickens for eggs. Of course, all this work had to be done at night after a long day in the fields, so they often gardened by the light of grease burning in an old skillet. When they could, they made their own food, such as kush, a cornmeal dish flavored

Slaves often had to provide for themselves. They might carve a bowl from a dried gourd or purchase an occasional piece of old silverware for the dinner table. Many plantation families, in contrast, sat down to lavish meals prepared and served by domestic servants.

Masters intentionally situated slave quarters away from the big house. At Boone Hall Plantation, a wall also separated the row of brick slave homes from the plantation gardens and mansion.

with onions and peppers and fried in a skillet. They also found ways to make their meals more like the spicy African food they remembered. Bland pork and stew became barbecue and gumbo, and slave cooks introduced okra and yams to the New World.

Masters typically situated cabins far from the big house to demonstrate that slaves were inferior beings, but the distance unintentionally offered the slaves a chance to have their own lives. Although in the masters' view slaves owned nothing and had no rights, the slaves themselves felt that their quarters belonged to them. Though they worked hard six days a week, they generally had the evenings and all day Sunday to themselves, so they readily formed their own society in their quarters. And there were many such communities. On the eve of the Civil War, in 1860, there were almost fifty thousand plantations with twenty or more slaves, home to nearly two thirds of America's two and a half million slaves, many of whom lived in communities the size of small villages. Living and working together, they looked to each other rather than the master for recognition, and they found their own leaders to resolve disputes and offer advice. The orator and former slave Frederick Douglass recalled that the slaves he had known in his days of captivity "were as true as steel, and no band of brothers could have been more loving. There were no mean advantages taken of each other, as is sometimes the case where slaves are situated as we were, no tattling; no giving each other bad names . . . and no elevating one at the expense of the other . . . We were generally a unit, and moved together."

Though their cabins were often drafty and crude, slaves worked hard to keep them clean and make them into homes for their families.

Slave communities were also held together by a rich social and cultural life. Old men, who were highly respected, told stories based on West African legends. Among the most popular were trickster

This 1862 photograph was taken by Timothy O'Sullivan on the J. J. Smith Plantation in Beaufort, South Carolina. Families gathered socially as often as they could.
Courtesy, Illinois State Historical Society

stories, in which a small animal outwits a more powerful one. Some of these stories survive in the tales of Uncle Remus. Slaves also told a group of stories about the never-ending struggles between the wise and strong slave John and Old Marster.

They recounted tales of Nat Turner, who led a slave revolt, and Harriet Tubman, who guided runaways to freedom on the Underground Railroad. Young people listened intently, not only because they loved the stories and were encouraged by their messages, but because they wanted to pass the stories

Slaves were merely possessions for their owners. These slave quarters were lined up in front of the main house and made out of brick to show off the plantation's wealth. Inside, the cabins were barren.

down to their own children and grandchildren someday.

Within the cabin walls, slaves also secretly taught each other to read and write, often late at night by the light of the fire. Fearing that education would lead to demands for human rights and to organized uprisings, many southern states passed laws forbidding slaves to be educated. Slaves who dared to read and write, even their own names, were whipped; some had their thumb or forefinger chopped off. Nonetheless, they persisted in teaching themselves, as the simple act of writing their names demonstrated that they had identities.

At night the quarters pulsed with the rhythm of people seeking release from everyday drudgery. In the early days of slavery, musicians played the qua-qua or the gudugudu, drums made from sections of hollowed-out tree trunks covered with animal skins. However, during the Stone insurrection of 1739, in which slaves rose up against their masters, slaves used drums to send messages to each other. After-ward, fearing that this would happen again, many masters outlawed drums. Slaves then duplicated the sound of drumbeats by stomping their feet and slap-ping their bodies. They also made sheep-hide ban-jos, gourd fiddles, mandolins or "molos," and Af-rican-style gourd rattles, as well as other instru-ments improvised from beef rib bones and willow stalks. Slave fiddlers and banjo pickers were often joined by singers and dancers. As one slave ex-plained, "Tain't no use o' sp'ilin' de Sat'day night by countin' de time to Monday mornin'." Long stretch-es of work in the fields and at quiltings and corn shucking were ended with get-togethers at which slaves sang and danced.

Despite mistreatment, hard work, and the ever-

The interior of this slave dwelling on Carter Grove Plantation in Virginia was once the scene of social gatherings at the end of each long day's work. Within these walls, slaves told stories, sang, and danced. Note the round fence—an African building style.

present threat of sale, slaves struggled to maintain families. They had to ask the master's permission to marry, but they generally chose their own partners. Sometimes formal weddings were held, even in the big house. However, masters were usually not comfortable with Christian weddings for slaves. The vow "Till death do us part" and the injunction "What God has joined together, let no man put asunder" went too clearly against the practice of slavery. Masters usually insisted on a simple "Now you're married." Yet a marriage was an occasion of great joy in the quarters, when a couple not only expressed their love for each other but publicly

Living together in large groups, often sharing food, clothing, and shelter, slaves had much in common, which helped them to create a strong sense of community.
Courtesy, J. Paul Getty Museum

bound themselves to the community. Despite sales, slave marriages lasted for many years, often a lifetime. Of her husband, one slave woman said, "He was the first one and the best one and the last one."

Children were often named after blood kin to strengthen a sense of extended family. They led difficult lives, but there was little sibling rivalry. Parents deeply cared for their young ones for as long as they could keep them and tried to protect them as much as possible from the hardships of the plantation. Fathers fascinated their children with stories and brought them small gifts. Although parents

weren't allowed much time with their children—
new mothers often had to take their babies to the
fields to nurse—they tried to bring them up with a
sense of dignity. Sara Colquitt explained, "Miss
Mary was good to us, but we had to work hard and
late. I worked in the fields every day from before
daylight to almost plumb dark. I used to take my lit-
tlest baby with me, and I'd tie it up to a tree limb to
keep off the ants and bugs whilst I hoed and worked
the furrow." Maintaining the sense of kinship in
African villages, slave families extended beyond the
immediate household to include grandparents,
aunts, uncles, cousins, and everyone in the community—and everyone cared for the children.

It is well known that the lives of the enslaved
were clearly defined by work, but only recently have
we realized how much plantation owners depended
on slaves as both field hands and skilled workers.
Men and women worked in the fields and in the
yard, an area near the big house that included the
kitchen, dairy, smokehouse, and well. It was here
that much of the household work was done. They
washed laundry, put up preserves, smoked meat
(mainly pork), and made candles and soap. Slave
carpenters, blacksmiths, coopers, and other skilled
people also worked in this area. Designed to keep
everything under the master's eye yet apart from the
lives of the owners, the yard had its own society. It
was full of conversation, laughter, and song as

In addition to cooking meals and washing clothes, slaves worked at many tasks, including spinning cotton into yarn, with which they made clothing for the master's family and themselves.

friends and family helped each other get through the day.

Domestic servants worked in the big house and often lived in separate cabins near the house and away from the quarters. Much of these slaves' work went on in the yard. The kitchen was typically separate from the main house because of its heat and noise, and also to show that even domestic servants were not of the same class as those who resided in the big house. Whether cooking, cleaning, or waiting on the master and his family, domestic servants didn't stop working at sundown. This small group of slaves— no more than a half-dozen even on the larger plantations—were on call both day and night. Yet they also knew what was happening in the big house and could warn those in the quarters of a coming sale or other danger.

Many slaves had been farmers in Africa, and their knowledge and ability was valued on the plantations. Slaves on rice plantations in the coastal areas of the Carolinas undertook the formidable tasks of draining marshes infested with mosquitoes and establishing irrigation systems. They carefully

tended the rice fields to keep a precise amount of water in them and to prevent the backup of salt water. Along with managing the irrigation canals, they ran the winnowing house, where the hard grain was separated from the hull.

Morning, noon, and night, slave women toiled before a fire in the kitchen hearth, where they ably cooked meals for the master's family. That family always ate better than the slaves and their husbands and children.

The sugar plantations of Louisiana resembled mills or factories: in the sweltering heat, teams of field hands chopped sugar canes, which were then hauled to the yard in carts so heavy they were often rolled on railroad tracks. With large presses, slaves squeezed the canes to get juice, which was then cooked down to sweet bubbly syrup and refined into sugar. During the harvest season, slaves worked long

Young and old, slaves worked with piles of cotton at the quarters, separating the fluffy white bolls from the leaves and stems. During the harvest, they worked well into the evening each and every day.
Courtesy, Illinois State Historical Society

into the night, often eighteen hours a day. Since the large barrels of sugar were best transported on boats, sugar plantations were usually located along the Mississippi River.

Cotton became the principal crop of the Deep South, including Texas, and the fluffy white bolls had to be tediously picked by hand. Even after the introduction of the cotton gin, a machine that separated the seeds from the cotton, many laborers were needed to harvest this crop. Slaves "ginned" the cotton to remove the seeds and leaves, often working until nine o'clock at night, and then pressed it into compact six-hundred-pound bales.

Tobacco was usually grown on smaller farms, and the delicate crop needed special attention from the time the individual plants were set out in the spring. Slaves continually weeded fields and removed worms by hand—and were cruelly punished if they missed any. Nancy Williams described how her master "picked up a hand full of worms, he did, an' stuffed 'em inter my mouth; Lordy knows how many of dem shiny things I done swallered, but I sho' picked 'em off careful arter that." Finally, the plants had to be harvested at just the right time or the leaves would be bitter. This made for long, hard hours in the fields. Gabe Hunt recalled, "Hands git so stuck up in dat old tobaccy gum it git so yo'

Cotton was so important to the economy of the South (and the textile mills of the North) that it became known as "King Cotton."

Alfred lived most of his life at the Hermitage. He was born a slave and died a slave, although Andrew Jackson thought so highly of him that he was buried in the Jackson family plot.

fingers stick together. Dat old gum was de worse mess you ever see. Couldn't brush it off, couldn't wash it off, got to wait till it wear off."

Although forced to work against their will, slaves took pride in their abilities. Since they planted, tended, and harvested the crops, they naturally felt that the cotton, rice, tobacco, and sugar belonged to them. Over time, some slaves became attached to the land as well. Morris, a freed slave from South Carolina, explained to his former master why he wished to continue to live on the plantation, saying, "I was born on dis place before Freedom. My Mammy and Daddy worked de rice fields. Dey's buried here. De fust ting I remember are dose rice banks. I growed up in dem from dat high . . . De strength of dese arms and dese legs and dis back . . . is in your rice banks."

Many slaves were highly skilled craftspeople. Slave blacksmiths not only shod horses but fashioned impressive wrought-iron gates and fences, notably in South Carolina and Louisiana. On rice plantations in South Carolina, slaves became renowned for their African style of coiled basketry, and African-American potters fashioned lovely stoneware. Women made articles for the household, and the quilts of Harriet Powers and the cross-stitch embroidery of Mamie Garvin Fields have come to be considered works of art.

Although owners usually didn't interfere in the social life of the quarters, they didn't want slaves wandering off the plantation either. So when slaves visited other plantations, they had to have a handwritten pass called a remit. If not, they could be stopped by groups of local police called patrollers or "patty-rollers." As the former slave Jane Pyatt recalled, "Sometimes the officials would beat them, and sometimes they would sell them. These patrollers took two of my brothers, one seven years old and the other five years old, and I have never seen either since. Where they were carried, none of our family has ever been able to find out." Yet slaves generally

In an attempt to maintain absolute control over their workers, some masters locked the cabins at night and fixed steel bars over the windows to keep slaves from visiting other plantations or running away.

Paths discovered on plantation grounds trace the routes slaves took at work and during precious free time when they stole away to secret meetings.

persisted in having their own lives, away from the prying eyes of the master. In particular, young men often went courting at other plantations, and if the master locked the cabins at night, they simply climbed out the chimney.

Courting wasn't the only reason for slipping away. Paths crisscrossed the plantation where slaves went back and forth not only to the fields and yard but also to secret places hidden deep in the woods. As one slave recalled, "Meetings back then meant more than they do now. Then everybody's heart was in tune, and when they called on God they made heaven ring." In keeping with an old African belief that a turned-over iron pot would capture secret conversations, Levi Pollard explained, "They always has a watcher to look out for pattyrollers. They turn a pot down so as not to let the sound go far." In some meetings slaves made plans to run away, while in others they plotted the end of slavery.

Many masters attempted to control their laborers through religion, but few slaves were fooled. As one man recounted, "The preacher came and he'd just say, 'Serve your masters. Don't steal your master's turkey. Don't steal your master's chickens . . . Do whatsomever your master tells you to do.' Same old thing all the time." Slaves embraced religion because through singing and preaching they were offered release from the hardships of bondage and hope for a better future. They identified with the tribes and clans of the Old Testament, especially those in the story of Exodus, and hoped that like the children of Israel, they would be liberated.

For most slaves, religion was a blend of Christianity and African beliefs in magic and herbal medicine, which was used by conjurers to cure everything from ills to curses. In the late eighteenth century, most slaves were converted to Christianity in revivals when the Baptists and the Methodists took an antislavery position, giving them hope for emancipation. African-American men were sometimes allowed to preach in their own churches as well,

Some masters required slaves to attend church services with them, although the slaves had to sit in the back pews or the choir loft of chapels like this one. Although many slaves converted to Christianity, they preferred their own churches and preachers.

and slaves much preferred their own services with their own preachers, clapping hands and singing spirituals or "sorrow songs." Even if they were required to attend services with whites, they had their own secret services in the quarters. Through spirituals they recounted their suffering but also looked forward to freedom, as when they sang, "There's a better day a-coming / Go sound the jubilee!" Many of these songs had hidden meanings; for instance, the promised land of Canaan was actually Canada, the destination of many runaways on the Underground Railroad.

Abolitionist efforts and the continual resistance

of the slaves themselves gradually weakened the peculiar institution of slavery, leading to the Civil War, which at long last destroyed the plantation system. It was another hundred years before African Americans began to have equal justice, but newly freed slaves could hope for a better future for themselves and their children.

Today, many African Americans view their ancestors not as slaves but as enslaved people who refused to accept their condition. Enslaved African Americans did indeed sustain their human dignity for themselves and as a legacy for their children.

Despite 250 years of enslavement, African Americans never gave up hope that they would someday be free. With the end of slavery, they began the struggle for equal justice as well.

When this photograph was taken outside a brick slave dwelling at the Hermitage in 1867, this woman had spent most of her life as a slave, but she could look forward to a better future for her great-grandchildren. Courtesy, The Hermitage, Nashville, Tennessee

Kidnapped Africans were among the first immigrants to set foot on the shores of North America, the only people brought as slaves, and among the last to taste freedom and equal justice. For this reason, of all Americans, slaves and their descendants, having come the longest distance, possibly embody the best hope that the American dream of life, liberty, and the pursuit of happiness may someday be achieved for all people. Religion, folklore, and a unique history, as well as an abiding respect for one another as human beings, are all central to the slave experience, and today African Americans can look back with respect on their ancestors, who wove the bright threads of their lives for all time into the fabric of America.

Further Reading

Many excellent books are available in libraries and bookstores for those who would like to read more about the lives of slaves in antebellum America. Along with primary sources, the following books were consulted in the preparation of this book.

Blassingame, John W. *The Slave Community: Plantation Life in the Antebellum South*. New York: Oxford University Press, 1979.

Campbell, Edward D. C., and Rice, Kim S. *Before Freedom Came: African-American Life in the Antebellum South*. Richmond, Va.: Museum of the Confederacy, and Charlottesville: University Press of Virginia, 1991.

Cornelius, Janet Duitsman. *"When I Can Read My Title Clear": Literacy, Slavery, and Religion in the Antebellum South*. Columbia: University of South Carolina Press, 1991.

Escott, Paul D. *Slavery Remembered: A Record of Twentieth-Century Slave Narratives*. Chapel Hill: University of North Carolina Press, 1979.

Genovese, Eugene D. *Roll, Jordan, Roll: The World the Slaves Made*. New York: Pantheon, 1974.

Hurmence, Belinda. *We Lived in a Little Cabin in the Yard*. Winston-Salem, N.C.: John F. Blair, 1994.

Johnson, Isaac. *Slavery Days in Old Kentucky* (facsimile of the 1901 edition). Canton, N.Y.: Friends of the Owen D. Young Library and the St. Lawrence County Historical Association, 1994.

Kolchin, Peter. *American Slavery: 1619–1877*. New York: Hill & Wang, 1993.

Mellon, James. *Bullwhip Days: The Slaves Remember*. New York: Weidenfeld & Nicolson, 1988.

Nichols, Charles H., ed. *Black Men in Chains*. New York: Lawrence Hill, 1972.

Owens, Leslie Howard. *This Species of Property: Slave Life and Culture in the Old South*. New York: Oxford University Press, 1976.

Vlach, John Michael. *Back of the Big House: The Architecture of Plantation Slavery*. Chapel Hill: University of North Carolina Press, 1993.

Wilson, Charles Reagan, and Ferris, William, eds. *Encyclopedia of Southern Culture*. Chapel Hill: University of North Carolina Press, 1993.

Only recently has it been recognized that African Americans took an active role on the plantations of the antebellum South and that their lives were interwoven with those of everyone in America, North and South, because everyone was in one way or another linked to the slave-based economy. Increasingly, historical sites are offering interpretive programs about African Americans, and these places are becoming less difficult to locate. The following books proved to be very helpful to me, and I recommend them to anyone wishing to visit plantations and other sites important in the history of African Americans.

Haskins, Jim, and Biondi, Joann. *Hippocrene U.S.A. Guide to Historical Black South: Historical Sites, Cultural Centers and Musical Happenings of the African-American South*. New York: Hippocrene Books, 1993.

Savage, Beth L. *African American Historic Places*. Washington, D.C.: Preservation Press, 1994.

Thum, Marcella. *Exploring Black America: A History and Guide*. New York: Atheneum, 1975.

———. *Hippocrene U.S.A. Guide to Black America*. New York: Hippocrene Books, 1991.